Scaredy C

2 **Scaredy Cat chased the mouse.**

The mouse chased Scaredy Cat.

Scaredy Cat chased the rabbit.

The rabbit chased Scaredy Cat.

Scaredy Cat chased the spider.

The spider chased Scaredy Cat.

Scaredy Cat chased the bird.

The bird chased Scaredy Cat.

"I'm scared!" said Scaredy Cat.

"Don't be scared of me!"
said the bird.

"Don't be scared of me!"
said the spider.

"Don't be scared of me!"
said the rabbit.

"Don't be scared of me!"
said the mouse.

"Don't be scared of me!"
said Scaredy Cat.